Get free publicity – then turn it into leads, sales, and extra cash

By
PR expert and former journalist
Paul Green

Published by

www.publicityheaven.com

First published in Great Britain in 2009 by
Publicity Heaven Ltd
1 The Old Dairy
Knuston Home Farm
Irchester
Northants
NN29 7EX

08452 303049
www.publicityheaven.com
hello@publicityheaven.com

ISBN 978-0-9562952-0-0

Printed in Great Britain by the MPG Books Group, Bodmin and King's Lynn

For Helen
Who makes all the hard work worthwhile

Contents

YOU CAN GET MORE MEDIA ATTENTION FOR YOUR BUSINESS THAN ANY PR AGENCY CAN

In my 13 year media career I met a lot of business owners who were desperate to get free publicity but hadn't a clue where to start.

They correctly recognised that being featured regularly in the media and branded an expert by journalists would give them a huge competitive advantage.

Often, they thought the answer was to hire an expensive PR agency that would churn out press releases on their behalf. WRONG!

See, just as the business owner was sitting at their desk wishing for media attention, I was sitting at my desk inside a newspaper or radio station scratching my head, wondering where the next story was going to come from...

Journalists are desperate for great stories. Their hunger is growing every day and becoming harder to satisfy.

The internet has made it easy to get lots of news and information on virtually any subject you are interested in. So to keep hold of their readers, listeners or viewers, journalists have to work harder to give them really relevant content – and more of it.

At the same time most media outlets are suffering from shrinking advertising revenues, resulting in tighter budgets and fewer staff to do more work.

This presents nothing but opportunity for you.

CHAPTER 1

By understanding the grim situation journalists are in, you can help them do their job... and get yourself some valuable free publicity along the way.

You don't need to be a "creative" person. And you don't need to be able to write press releases (although they are still a powerful and useful tool).

All you need to be able to do is find the great stories hidden in your business – or easily generate powerful new stories. Talking to journalists and getting publicity is easy when you get the basics right.

I set up Publicity Heaven in 2005 to help business owners get free publicity quickly and easily, and then leverage it to grow their business.

As a journalist I saw all the bad, lazy things some PR agencies did on behalf of their clients. And I knew they often charged thousands of pounds a month for inexperienced junior staff to (badly) execute really basic PR strategies.

Often they failed to get significant media coverage, just because they didn't really understand what journalists wanted and how to give it to them.

By reading this book you will start to develop the ability to do a better job yourself.

It is packed with insider information on how you can get free publicity for your business, and then use it to generate leads, sales and extra cash.

Good luck – and I look forward to opening a magazine or switching on a TV news bulletin and seeing your business featured soon.

Paul Green, Publicity Heaven

THE DIFFERENCE BETWEEN PUBLICITY AND ADVERTISING

Let's start at the beginning. Public relations or PR is any communication between your business and the public.

If you write a letter to apologise to an unhappy customer, that's public relations (and these days, that letter could end up on someone's blog or website).

If your business sponsors a local Scout troop to do a litter pick, that's public relations.

Publicity is one element of public relations, where your communication is done through the media. Note that it's called free publicity because the media talks about your business for free. If you have to pay in any way, it's called advertising.

The advantage of advertising is that you have very high control over what is said about your business. After all, you are paying for the space. But that control comes with a high price – very low credibility.

In this media savvy world where we all have commercial messages thrown at us every day, we have learnt to ignore most paid advertisements. We know that when we see an advert, the person has paid to place that message.

Publicity is exactly the opposite. It has very high credibility because it is a journalist saying things about your business, and you can't pay them to do that. But of course it has very low control. You can influence what a journalist says, but you can't control it.

You can use free publicity for many things:

- Generate leads and convert them into paying customers more easily (many PR people disagree with this... but they're wrong)

- Build brand awareness

- Drive traffic to your website

- Stand out in a crowded marketplace

- Change perceptions about your business

- Educate or influence people (including potential customers)

- Give your business credibility

- Make sure lots of people hear your good stories

- Generate word of mouth publicity

- Deal with a crisis

THE 5 UNBREAKABLE RULES OF FREE PUBLICITY

It is simple to get free publicity. In fact, the reason that many businesses get it wrong is because they try to overcomplicate things.

Ever heard of KISS? It stands for Keep It Simple... Stupid. No offence intended. It's a phrase that almost could have been designed for PR.

There are five powerful and unbreakable rules you should follow when trying to get free publicity:

1. Know your target audience and deliver to it:

Journalists are ultra focused on their audience. If the people they are creating content for want to know about a specific subject, that's what they will write about. If you turn up wanting to get publicity about something else, they won't be interested. You need to understand exactly what your target audience is interested in, and ensure your story suggestions fit within that. Get that right and it becomes a lot easier to persuade journalists to run your stories.

2. Be so different that you naturally catch the attention of journalists:

Any business that enjoys a certain degree of commercial success has differentiated itself from its competitors. And it's no different when you pursue free publicity. Your story suggestions need to be packed with "standoutability" (a made up word that sums it up perfectly). Journalists get hundreds of press releases and story suggestions every day... if yours are the same as all the others, they're going to go the same way (the bin).

3. Position yourself as an expert

This is the single most powerful idea in publicity. If journalists know you're an expert in your field, they'll turn to you first, time and time again, for information and comment on your industry. And that means your customers will know you're an expert too. Incidentally, it doesn't really matter who is the one true expert in your industry... it matters more who positions themselves first to the journalists and their audience.

4. Give journalists what they want and need, when they want and need it

99% of press releases sent to journalists go straight in the bin (these days they hit the delete key on their computer keyboard, often without even opening and reading the email you sent them). It's because the people who write them don't understand what journalists want, so can't give it to them. You have the opportunity to be in the one per cent who knows what journalists want and give it to them time and time again. Once you do have a journalist interested in your business, ensure you give them what they ask for quickly and efficiently. It's possible to lose media attention as quickly as you attracted it just because you're not helping the journalist do their job. Journalists are just like your customers. If you don't fill their needs when they want them filled, they will go elsewhere.

5. Generate creative and imaginative story ideas

Getting publicity is great fun and can invigorate you and your team! But it doesn't have to be difficult. Yes you need to be creative and generate new ideas. Actually, there are several easy ways to do this... including some "cheats", and it doesn't matter whether you consider yourself to be creative or not. There are systems and strategies to help you generate new ideas simply and easily.

CHAPTER 3

21 KILLER IDEAS FOR FREE PUBLICITY

Some ideas are so powerful that they generate publicity for businesses year after year after year.

In my 13 year media career I kept seeing variations of these ideas come up, and kept giving free publicity to the businesses behind them!

You can use any of these to generate free publicity for your business.

1. Be the first, the newest, the oldest, the biggest, the smallest

Different is great. Journalists get sent a constant stream of "average" all day long - so make sure you stand out.

2. Introduce something new or improved

Make it clear what's better and why, and what problem it solves.

3. Mark the passage of time

Has it been a year, 5 years, or 10 years since something significant happened?

4. Announce a new member of your team

Doesn't have to be anyone senior, even junior staff can sometimes get attention. Pinpoint the thing that made them the right person for the job and publicise that.

5. Win an award

Don't just rely on publicity sent by the award organisers, send out your own.

6. Win a big contract

Don't be afraid to boast – big contracts attract other big contracts.

7. React to a current story

Give your opinion on something in the news (national or local) that's relevant to you.

8. Offer free information

The years of experience you have in your industry makes you an expert. Journalists and readers appreciate an expert's opinion.

9. Give something free to readers

If you have an actual product or a book like this, give that away. You can use it to drive traffic from the newspaper to your website. Consider an exclusive deal with one media outlet to get more coverage.

10. Offer a series of articles

Share your expertise and help a newspaper or magazine fill column inches with interesting new content. Don't worry too much about your writing skills; they employ sub-editors to worry about that.

11. Survey your customers

Find out what people think about specific issues (related to your business). Ask enough of their target audience, and the media won't be able to resist.

12. Get involved with a charity

Don't just give cash, that's dull (plus cheque presentation photos are stuck in the 1980s). Instead give your time or product, or better still use your staff and resources to do something exciting and different that will also raise cash for an exciting charity.

13. Solve a problem
What's everyone talking about? What can you do to fix it?

14. Create a problem
Can you make things better by rocking the boat?

15. Do something in a different way
Particularly if it has "always been done this way". That's what Richard Branson and Stelios do.

16. Spot a trend and comment on it
Turn yourself into a commentator on a specific problem or industry.

17. Be anti-corporate
Journalists get a constant stream of boring, predictable corporate press releases. Be anti-corporate. Don't be afraid to stand out.

18. Be refreshingly honest
If you expose the hidden secrets of your industry, will you get the credit for that? The internet is making it easier than ever to find out what's really happening inside an industry. Will you lead the change or follow it?

19. Attempt to set or beat a record
A publicity classic, for a reason. Everyone loves a record attempt. And there are plenty to go for. Ensure your record is relevant in some way to your business.

20. Read the papers or websites for a month
Cut out / bookmark stories that catch your attention. Re-read all your clippings at the end of the month – what common themes or story ideas jump out at you? Or what are missing?

CHAPTER 4

21. Put on a publicity stunt

Such as dressing up your staff in tuxedos to celebrate a new James Bond film (this would be more effective the scruffier your staff normally are). Stunts should be fun for staff and customers as well as the media, and always be visually appealing.

GET THE STORY BASICS RIGHT

To get free publicity all you have to do is suggest a story to the media. If they think their audience will be interested in it, they will write about it. Simple.

But you need to make sure you are always giving the full story. If you miss a critical part of it out you will struggle to communicate your story properly.

Understanding this and getting it right will actually help all areas of your business marketing. Potential customers will feel that something isn't quite right when a part of the story is missing.

To ensure you are getting every part of your story and message across, you just need to answer these five questions:

Who
Who is this story about?
For example, Paul Green of Publicity Heaven.

What
What have they done or are they going to do?
Paul has written a book about how business owners can get free publicity.

Where
Where did this happen?
At Paul's office in Northamptonshire.

When
When did this happen?
In 2009.

CHAPTER 5

Why

This is the most important question of all. The other questions are mostly basic info – but the reason why someone is going to do something often IS the story. Sometimes, you may have to answer How something is being done as well.

Paul wrote this book because as a former journalist, he is passionate about helping business owners get free publicity for themselves.

WRITE A PRESS RELEASE (AKA MAKE A STORY SUGGESTION)

There is a myth that to get PR coverage you need to write press releases. Scrub that from your mind right now.

Press releases are a **tool** of public relations and nothing more.

Simply writing a press release and sending it out won't get you media coverage. But if you create a press release that is used as a tool to communicate a great story to a journalist... now that's a different matter.

It's just like when you are selling things in your business. If you have something that people really really want, it doesn't matter if your website isn't quite right or your sales letters aren't particularly effective. These things will diminish your sales, but they won't affect the basic demand for your product.

It's the same in PR. If you have a relevant story packed with standoutability, journalists will want it. Not being able to write a press release may make it slightly harder for you to communicate the story, but ultimately if it's good enough, journalists will want it anyway.

The most reliable way to communicate a story to a journalist is to pick up the phone and talk to him or her. It takes more time, but it can generate the best results.

You also need to be able to communicate your story suggestion in written form. That could be through a press release or maybe just in an email. This is because most journalists like to see a written version of a story you are suggesting.

Whether you are putting together a press release or a simple email, here are the basic elements you need.

An attention catching headline

Just as newspapers use a great headline to catch attention, you've got to do the same with your press release or email.

A good opening paragraph

News editors or journalists will decide whether to run the story - or bin the press release - on the strength of the headline and opening paragraph.

Main body

Here's where you spell out your story, using the 5 unbreakable rules of free publicity. And make sure you give the whole story: who, what, where, when, why.

Use a quote where you can

People like reading about people. So give a quote from someone commenting on the story. Keep it to one person if possible.

At the end, write a section called Notes to editors

This is the place to give journalists information that you don't necessarily want to see published. Give them your contact details in case they want to arrange a photo or do an interview with you. You should always have a spokesperson available.

PASS THE "SO WHAT?" TEST

When a journalist first looks at your story suggestion or press release, they will ask themselves one question: So what?

What they mean is, "how is this relevant to the audience I am writing for?"

If your story doesn't answer this question in seconds, it will be deleted.

It's a great idea to get a colleague - or better someone with no emotional investment in your business - to look over your story suggestion before you send it.

Here are a series of questions to ask yourself.

Do you know what you want to achieve with your publicity?

Does it fit with your business goal? No point getting publicity for the sake of it, you should be clear what you want to achieve.

Have you told the whole story?

Have you remembered who, what, where, when - and most importantly why?

Can your target audience relate to it?

If you want to reach 35 year old housewives, a story about classic cars probably won't appeal to the majority of them. Ideally you should show your story to someone in your target audience, to see if they are interested.

Is it a good enough story?

Have you got enough standoutability built in? Examine the media you want to get publicity with. Is your story as good as, or better than the stories they are already carrying? Being ordinary isn't enough, you must stand out.

Are you giving the journalist everything they want?

Make it easy for them, and you will get more publicity.

SEND IT TO THE RIGHT JOURNALISTS

Most journalists prefer receiving press releases and story suggestions by email. Even if you speak to them on the phone, they will normally ask you to email the details over.

Never send Word attachments unless specifically asked. Instead copy and paste your press release into the body of your email.

If you must email press releases to several journalists at once, make sure you either send them one at a time, or put all the email addresses into the BCC field. Better still use an email marketing tool such as Sign-up.to or Constant Contact.

Here's how to build a powerful media list in just 15 minutes.

Decide which media sector your target audience consumes
For local people it will be the local media; for plumbers it would be their trade press.

Find out the names of all your target media outlets
Look in newsagents or do a Google search.

Find the outlets' websites
The easiest way is to consume the media (read the magazine, listen to the radio station). Alternatively you can use Google, or a handy resource such as www.MediaUK.com.

Look for the most relevant contact details
A general email address, such as news@newspapertitle.co.uk is OK. Ideally you will find the contact details of the specific journalist who is most likely to be interested in your story.

CHAPTER 8

TRACK THE MEDIA COVERAGE YOUR BUSINESS GETS

Remember, there's no guarantee any journalist will use your press release. It's a key component of publicity - minimum control but maximum credibility (compared to the maximum control and minimum credibility of paid-for advertising).

You won't always know when a journalist writes a story about your business. Sometimes they will copy and paste a few lines straight into their publication – that's why if you do send a press release you need to follow a common format (press releases are written in the same style as news stories).

The journalist doesn't have to ask you or tell you if they do this. By sending a press release or email, you give them the right to copy and adapt your story suggestion.

If you are particularly active it would be worth you hiring a media monitoring company. They will read 5,000 publications a week looking out for mentions of your business.

Expect to pay a couple of hundred pounds a month for this service. You will also need a license from the Newspaper Licensing Association, to ensure you don't break any copyright laws.

While it's vital you track what is being written about your business (so you can use it to generate leads and sales), you can do this yourself.

There are a number of DIY options you can use to track your coverage.

Set up Google Alerts

As Google searches the internet for new content, it can email you an alert every time it finds your business or product name on any website or blog. Go to www.google.co.uk/alerts. You don't need a Google account to set up an alert. Simply enter the terms you want to be alerted for, and your email address. Google will send a confirmation email you need to click on.

To ensure you are fully covered, set up several alerts to cover every way your business might be written about. For example, you might have "Business Name" (in quotes) to cover the business name, but also "businessname" to cover the website address.

SUCCESS TIP Set up Google Alerts on your competitors' names, so you always know what they are up to.

Use WatchThatPage

There is a website at www.WatchThatPage.com that will monitor websites and email you when a page is changed. This is an ideal way of monitoring media websites that don't change more than once or twice a week.

Get the RSS or Twitter feed

Most websites have RSS feeds. It stands for Really Simple Syndication, and is a feed of headlines from the site. You can monitor all the headlines from several different sites without having to visit them. All you need is an RSS Reader. Google that term or use a service like www.Protopage.com. Alternatively many media titles now feed their stories through Twitter (www.Twitter.com).

Consume the media

The old fashioned way of checking for coverage, but the most efficient - particularly if you are after publicity in your local area.

SUCCESS TIP Put a value on your PR coverage. Big companies measure the AVE, or Advertising Value Equivalent of their PR coverage. That means, if you had to pay for the space you got, how much would it have cost you?

A full page in a daily newspaper can cost upwards of £20,000 – not bad for an investment of an hour of your time in PR. You can often find out the cost of a page on the media outlet's website.

GET READY TO DO MEDIA INTERVIEWS

If your press release is highly successful, you will get some journalists ringing you up asking for an interview.

Don't panic! Unless you are a politician, they are probably not out to "get you". Instead they just want to add a little colour to the story that you have sent them, and get some new quotes from you (or sound bites if it's a radio station).

Here are a few basic tips to ensure you are ready.

Be prepared
Re-read your press release or story suggestion and make sure you have swotted up on the subject matter. Don't go over the top - compared to the journalist and most people, you ARE an expert in your subject. Sounding confident will take you a long way.

Anticipate possible questions
And prepare possible answers if you need to. But be very aware of trying to guess every question and then read answers off a sheet. Not only will this damage your confidence, but you will sound false with your answers. Trust the expertise you have in your head.

Practice with a friend
Give them your story suggestion and get them to ask you questions about the story.

CHAPTER 10

THE BIGGEST PR MISTAKES MADE BY BUSINESS OWNERS

Getting free publicity is powerful and easy. I hope the information in this book has proved that to you.

While I was a journalist, I saw business owners (and PR agencies) make the same three basic mistakes time and time again.

Don't make these mistakes in your business:

1) You don't generate good enough stories

Sorry, but journalists don't care about you or your business. They only care about stories that are of interest to their audience. It can be very dull being a journalist, wading through the same old stuff being sent to you day in, day out. So when something special comes along you jump on it. As a business owner, that's your opportunity.

2) You give up after one press release

If you send out 100 direct mail letters and then stop because "direct mail doesn't work for you", then you are missing out on a huge opportunity. It's not that direct mail doesn't work for you… you just haven't found the right way to make it work for you yet. PR is exactly the same. There is no way that every press release you ever send or every story suggestion you make to a journalist will be picked up and turned into free publicity. You have to make a long-term commitment. The advice in this book will make your PR much more relevant.

3) You don't get the right kind of mentions in the media and then use that coverage to generate leads

PR is not really meant as a direct lead generation tool (although many businesses find it does work that way). It can certainly be used to enhance the credibility of your business and support the rest of your marketing. You need to make sure that the media coverage received by your business makes it really easy for interested readers, listeners or viewers to find you. And then that coverage must be made to work to help generate leads and convert prospects into customers for months and years to come.

GET POWERFUL FREE PUBLICITY IN THE MEDIA FOR YOUR BUSINESS IN JUST 28 DAYS... OR LESS

I hope the contents of this book have been useful to you. Now I have some questions to ask...

Are you ready to turn your business into a PR machine that generates plenty of valuable free publicity all year round with very little effort?

Are you open to learning powerful but simple insider strategies that have been proven to generate PR coverage time and time again?

Would you like to wake up in the morning and find your business has attracted free publicity without you having lifted a finger?

And would you be delighted to see that publicity attract new leads and make prospective clients say "yes" more quickly, beating your competitors?

If the answer to these questions is "yes" then say yes once more and join me as I spill my detailed insider secrets.

This is your personal invitation to learn the secrets PR agencies don't want you to know

I'm not going to be popular among my PR agency peers for creating the success programme I'm going to tell you about. The secrets I'll be revealing are heavily guarded – and no wonder. They are so simple to use that many big agencies get inexperienced junior staff to execute them, while the directors sit at the top and get rich.

My experience as a journalist and PR insider has convinced me that my belief is true:

"Any business can attract free publicity quickly and very easily"

But most businesses don't bother. That's crazy! Most businesses need the credibility of free publicity as a powerful and highly cost effective marketing tool, to ward off bigger competitors with larger marketing budgets.

In my 13 year career as a newspaper journalist, news editor and radio presenter, I kept meeting business owners who were grateful to get free publicity – but didn't understand why I had picked some stories and not others.

And because they didn't understand it, they couldn't generate MORE stories to get even more free publicity... even though I was desperate for story ideas.

This is what drove me to set up Publicity Heaven. I wanted to help businesses grow using free publicity.

I could see businesses spending thousands of pounds on PR agencies that didn't really care about the results.

Why would you do that? The truth is that no-one can do PR for your business better than you and your team.

And here's the best bit:

You don't even need to be "creative" or know how to write!

Getting free publicity is all about having a bit of knowledge and following simple rules. Since setting up Publicity Heaven in 2005, I've used those rules time and time again to generate hundreds of thousands of pounds of free publicity for my clients.

Last year I got an IT company on page 3 of the Daily Star (they were delighted)... then a few months later they were on page 3 of Metro and in the Daily Telegraph.

I got a health and safety company onto national radio and into a number of magazines, then helped them use that free publicity to generate powerful sales leads (that were much easier to convert than cold leads).

One start-up paid me £2,000 to help them launch their business. Three days later they were in all the national newspapers and on BBC News 24. The coverage was worth in excess of £100,000. Even though they got a Return on Investment of FIFTY TIMES what they paid, I still felt guilty, because it took just 30 minutes' work to get that coverage.

Here is what some of my clients have said over the years:

An unbelievable media response: *"We've received incredible press coverage, ranging from national newspapers, to local newspapers and radio stations. In fact, the response was so good that at times I struggled to find the time to fit in all the interview requests from the media!"*
Charles Cridland, YourParkingSpace.co.uk

Widespread coverage: *"It is a challenge to get exposure, notice and coverage in a competitive market, but we managed to get widespread media coverage including newspapers, magazines, online and radio stations."*
Janine Sinclair, froggybank.co.uk

National exposure: *"Within weeks of working with Publicity Heaven we featured in the Daily Mirror and the Guardian."*
Chrissie Lewis, SingleWithKids.co.uk

The staff love it: *"T-Enterprise is now a company that talks regularly to national journalists/radio DJs. Also our staff have become more passionate in their work from the national exposure they have been enjoying!"*
Zarrar Chishti, T-Enterprise

Half a million pounds of coverage: *"We estimate that Paul and his PR team have generated for us £500,000 of 'free' publicity including radio, local and national press, and national and international TV coverage."*
Andrew McGavin, BetterDrivingPlease.com

While it has been extremely rewarding helping these clients, it has also been frustrating meeting so many small business owners who need help like this – and could turn their PR into extra profits – but just can't afford to pay a PR agency.

So I've decided to lay out my techniques in a detailed and focused five part programme to show business owners just how easy it is to get their own free publicity. I'm going to reveal the things that have taken me years to learn and perfect.

These are just 7 of the powerful PR techniques you will learn...

1. How to find out when journalists are most open to your story suggestions

2. How to find out exactly which media your target customers use (meaning you know exactly how to get a powerful sales message in front of them)

3. The easy way to generate an unlimited number of stories, even if you consider yourself not to be a "creative" person

4. The small details that make a difference to the amount of coverage you will get

5. The number one thing journalists hate and how to get round it

6. The specific tools used by top PR agencies – including three that are totally free

7. The biggest mistake made by businesses that cripples their PR – and how to avoid it

The PR Success Programme will help you bring the power of unlimited free publicity to your business

We all know the importance of taking time out to work "on" your business rather than "in" it, but rarely do it.

This is your invitation to take a few hours to work through a powerful programme and learn valuable secrets that will generate free publicity and potential profits for years to come.

The PR Success Programme has been put together by me as a comprehensive guide to generate free publicity for your business in 28 days or less. And not just free publicity for the sake of it – it is PR coverage that will help your business achieve its goals.

This isn't a dusty book full of dull PR theory. This is an easy to use audio programme (with full transcripts) focused on practical actions that work.

Here are a few more of thing things you will learn:

• The crucial difference between PR and advertising

- Exactly what journalists are looking for in story suggestions and how to communicate them

- Why a press release is a powerful tool – and why it doesn't matter if you "can't write"

- 50 great ideas to generate stories for your business

- The enhancing factors that can get you more media coverage, no matter what the story

- The times of the year when it is easiest to get free publicity (there are 5 or 6 of them)

So here's another question for you...

If you're serious about learning how to create an unlimited avalanche of free publicity for your business, how much would all that advice and practical experience be worth to you?

Here's what you get with the PR Success Programme:

- 5 audio modules on three CDs (each module lasts just under 30 minutes), ready for you to listen to in the car, at work, or rip to your iPod

- An A4 manual with full transcripts of the 5 modules

- 50 story ideas that you can use in your business immediately

- A fourth CD containing PR templates you can use immediately, including a press release template (and a real life press release that generated media coverage); a template for a media factfile; and a handy document on how to spot a PR opportunity

If I said this could all be yours for just £197 + vat, what would you say?

Buy the PR Success Programme now at www.publicityheaven.com/prsuccessprogramme. But wait... there's more.

FREE BONUS NUMBER 1

How about if I give you a free DVD with my video "How to Write a Press Release", worth £47. In just 30 minutes you will learn:

- The most important element of any press release

- The easy way to write a press release headline that is perfect every time

- Why 99% of press releases are binned by news editors immediately... and how to make sure yours survives

- Why you must never send a Word document to journalists

FREE BONUS NUMBER 2

I'll also give you an additional bonus audio module called How To Be A Media Expert, worth £30.

Ever noticed that you seem to see the same people on TV and in newspapers time and time again? They've learnt the simple and clever techniques to position themselves to the media as the expert in their field.

It's not difficult, but it is a powerful way to get free publicity. And the best bit is you get journalists coming to you and asking for help.

This bonus audio module is a 30 minute interview I did with Bob Mills, the editor of ExpertSources.co.uk. After a long career as a journalist he now helps more than 1,000 experts get free publicity from more than 4,000 journalists. And in this fascinating interview, he reveals the secrets that his most active experts use to get publicity time and time again.

I'm not done yet, because thanks to Bob's generosity I can offer you...

FREE BONUS NUMBER 3

You'll also get a substantial 33% discount off an executive entry to Bob's database of media experts at ExpertSources.co.uk. He'll reveal how to see the specific things journalists are searching his database for, what that means, and how to use it to your advantage.

Your 33% discount is strictly open to PR Success Programme customers only.

FULL 30 DAY MONEY BACK GUARANTEE

I'm so confident that this product is going to change your life that I'll put my money where my mouth is.

If you buy the PR Success Programme, listen to it and read the manual, and then decide you can't use any of the advice to get free publicity for your business; just return everything to me within 30 days – that's the audio CDs, written manual, CD of templates, bonus audio module and bonus DVD with ExpertSources.co.uk discount voucher – and I'll refund your money. Every single penny returned, no quibbles, guaranteed.

There is no risk for you. If you think the PR Success Programme contains business-changing advice and guidance, keep it and use it as your guide. If you don't, return it within 30 days and get all your money back, guaranteed.

Secure your copy of the PR Success Programme today

To help you generate free publicity in 28 days or less, here's a recap of what you get:

- 5 audio modules on three CDs

- A manual with full transcripts of the 5 modules

- A bonus 6th audio module "How To Be A Media Expert"

- 50 story ideas that you can use in your business immediately

- PR templates you can use immediately, contained on a handy CD

- Bonus DVD "How To Write A Press Release"

- Exclusive 33% discount off executive membership to the powerful ExpertSources.co.uk database

All this for just £197 plus vat.

Secure your copy now at www.publicityheaven.com/prsuccessprogramme.

It will be posted to you immediately.

Good luck

Any business – including yours – can get valuable free publicity and use it to generate leads, sales and profits.

I wish you the best of luck and look forward to seeing your business featured in the media soon.

Yours,

Paul Green

Paul Green
PublicityHeaven.com

P.S. Remember, there's zero risk buying the PR Success Programme consisting of 5 audio modules, full printed transcripts manual, CD of useful templates, bonus 6th module and bonus DVD, for £197 plus vat.

If you listen to the CDs, read the manual and decide it's not for you, just return it within 30 days for a full refund.

Don't put this to one side and do it later. Take action now to generate valuable free publicity for your business in 28 days or less at www.publicityheaven.com/prsuccessprogramme.

Gives you ideas: *"I found Paul to be very informative and has given me lots of ideas that I can implement to give me an edge over my competitors."*
Julie Futcher, HRGO Recruitment

Will be a media expert now: *"Very thought provoking, don't know why I didn't think of some of the points for effective public relations before. Will now make sure that any relevant news to our industry is followed up with comments from an expert. Ten out of ten."*
Pauline Holloway, Vulcan Fire Training

Return on investment: *"Very fast-paced and informative. Full of useful tips. I've adopted a couple of your hints and got a trial to write a weekly blog for an American newsletter called Innovation Tools."*
Paul Forsythe, Alemare Solutions

Endorsed by other marketing experts: *"Even though I've been involved in PR for many years, I picked up some useful tips, particularly for attracting radio. 8 out of 10."*
Karen Mahoney, Market Energy

Makes the difficult seem simple: *"I will certainly start work on my PR plan. What previously appeared a complex topic I know now to be relatively simple."*
Michael Markham, Michael Markham Mentoring & Motivational Speaking

Lots of tips and resources: *"Paul crunched the effective public relations knowledge into easily absorbed chunks. He also provided lots of free tips and resources that will be priceless for me. A definite 8 out of 10 - only because I want more!"*
Shelley Pearson, ExpertFranchiseGuide.com

Manage the **PR** **Power** of Your Staff

Employees are active spokespeople for an organisation. They have the power to affect, either positively or negatively, how a company or brand is viewed by its audiences and stakeholders.

This is most acute when companies go through change. Change is the essence of survival, but often employees are resistant to it or they simply don't understand what's happening and why. How you manage change will have a major impact on the PR generated by your staff.

Good PR – for free

Frequently, when companies make changes that are perceived as negative, such as redundancies, they fail to communicate their plans for the future. Remaining staff need to know the shape, size and direction in which the business is moving to keep them engaged, motivated and loyal.

Spirit HR can help you manage internal PR in times of change and seize a golden opportunity to pitch the positive future of the business – then have that message communicated onward by staff to their friends and family.

Bad PR – also for free!

Poor or unlawful handling of HR matters can lead to employers facing accusations such as unfair dismissal, bullying or discrimination in employment courts. Because any matters that go through the courts become public information, your local newspaper or trade magazine will gladly pick up any story of an employer being found (suspected or accused of) treating staff unlawfully.

While the awards against employers, if found against them, can be hefty and run into the thousands of pounds, the negative PR spread by former and existing employees, ably assisted by the press, can do untold damage to a business.

For advice on how to map a path to good PR through your staff communication strategy, or how to avoid the negative cost of headlining at employment tribunal for treating your staff unlawfully contact Spirit HR on enquiries@spirit-hr.co.uk or 01604 761 895.

To book a FREE 20 minute call to discuss your employment challenges quote PHS/SHR-09.

Direct Mailing Expert Reveals 10 Rarely Used Secrets to Increasing Mailing Response

Yes at last I can reveal the 10 secrets to direct mail that if followed will allow you to generate more response to your mailings but without spending a single penny more than you do now.

I have collected together for you the ten most powerful tips that your competitors do not want you to know.

On this **FREE** audio MP3 you discover:

- How to determine who to write to
- How to trim your mailings costs whilst still generating the highest impact
- The single, most effective thing you can do to make sure your message is read
- Why the wrong presentation of your mailing can decimate response
- Why using the wrong addressing method can drastically cut your open rate.

These tips really are **FREE** and you will also receive a tip sheet which contains additional sources of information that help you maximise your direct mail.

Successful Results

Paul Green , Publicity Heaven said
" The audio is very informative and should be listened to be anyone wanting better response from their direct mail"

Get The Facts FREE

Remember, the 10 Secrets to Effective Direct Mail doesn't cost you a single penny but could save you hundreds in mailing costs and generate thousands in new business.

Act quickly and take advantage of this offer by simply visiting

www.directmailtips.co.uk

Pop your details onto the form and your free MP3 will be on its way!

As a special bonus you will also receive the second MP3 of more tips on its release FREE of charge.